GEOMETRY'S GREAT THINKERS

The History of Geometry

Bonnie Coulter Leech

PowerMath™

The Rosen Publishing Group's

PowerKids Press™
New York

Published in 2007 by The Rosen Publishing Group, Inc.
29 East 21st Street, New York, NY 10010

Copyright © 2007 by The Rosen Publishing Group, Inc.

Book Design: Michael J. Flynn

Photo Credits: Cover (Descartes, Pythagoras), pp. 10, 14 © Bettmann/Corbis; cover (backgrounds) ©
Photodisc; pp. 5 (Egyptian fresco), 16 © Archivo Iconografico, S.A./Corbis; pp. 5 (map of the world stone),
© The Bridgeman Art Library/Getty Images; p. 9 © Eyewire; pp. 17, 21 © Hulton Archive/Getty Images; p. 18
© Araldo de Luca/Corbis; p. 22 © Kean Collection/Getty Images; p. 25 © Stapleton Collection/Corbis; p. 26
© Angelo Hornak/Corbis; p. 30 © Joseph Sohm; ChromoSohm Inc./Corbis.

Leech, Bonnie Coulter.
   Geometry's great thinkers : the history of geometry / Bonnie Coulter Leech.
      p. cm. — (Math for the real world)
   Includes index.
   ISBN 1-4042-3360-1 (library binding)
   ISBN 1-4042-6073-0 (pbk.)
   6-pack ISBN 1-4042-6074-9
   1. Geometry—History—Juvenile literature. 2. Geometry—Problems, Famous—History—Juvenile literature.
3. Mathematicians—History—Juvenile literature. I. Title. II. Series.
   QA445.5.L446 2006
   516—dc22
                                        2005014937

Manufactured in the United States of America

CONTENTS

ANCIENT GEOMETRY 4

THALES OF MILETUS 11

PYTHAGORAS OF SAMOS 15

EUCLID OF ALEXANDRIA 20

RENÉ DESCARTES 23

GRACE CHISHOLM YOUNG 27

THE PIONEERS OF GEOMETRY 30

GLOSSARY 31

INDEX 32

ANCIENT GEOMETRY

What is geometry? Geometry is the branch of mathematics that deals with the measurements, properties, and relationships of points, lines, planes, and solids. The word "geometry" comes from the Greek words *geo* and *met*, meaning "earth measuring."

In ancient Babylon and Egypt, geometry grew out of the need to make measurements involving farmland, crops, trade, and construction. From about 2000 B.C. to 1600 B.C., ancient Babylonians used geometry to find the lengths, widths, and diagonals of rectangles. They were familiar with general rules for finding the area of a rectangle and the areas of triangles, including **right triangles** and **isosceles triangles**. They also knew how to find the radius of a circle and the areas of regular **polygons** with 3 to 7 sides.

In ancient Babylon, the standard units for measurement were the *kush* for length, the *sar* for area and volume, the *sila* for capacity, and the *mana* for weight. The system was based on the barleycorn, or *she*. This was the smallest unit of length, area, volume, and weight. One barleycorn is about $\frac{1}{360}$ meter, or 0.11 inch.

Like the Babylonians, Egyptians created measurement formulas to compute land areas and crop volumes, and to aid in construction. Ancient Egyptians knew that the area of any triangle is $\frac{1}{2}$ the product of the base times the height. They also knew how to calculate the volume of a pyramid.

In this book, we will look at the development of geometry from ancient to modern times, as well as the contributions of some famous mathematicians.

This early map, created around 600 B.C., shows the world as a circle and Babylon as a rectangle crossed by the Euphrates and Tigris Rivers. This ancient map shows that the Babylonians used geometry to describe their world.

5

Babylonian and Egyptian knowledge of geometry was based on practical experience. There is evidence that they established the framework that inspired Greek geometry. Let's take a look at a few of the geometric rules we use today that were known by the ancient Babylonians and Egyptians.

A circle is the set of all points in a plane that are an equal distance from a given point, called the center. A radius is a line segment that has 1 endpoint at the center of the circle and the other endpoint on the circle itself. The diameter of a circle is a line segment that has both endpoints on the circle and goes through the center point.

The ratio of the **circumference** of a circle to its diameter is always the same number, no matter what size the circle is. That number is called pi (π). We can write this relationship as an equation: circumference divided by diameter equals pi, or $\frac{c}{d} = \pi$. We can also write this formula as $C = \pi d$. Even in ancient times, Egyptians and Babylonians knew the ratio was always the same, although they did not know the value of that number as precisely as we do today. The Egyptians calculated pi to be about 3.160484. The Babylonians estimated it to be about 3.125. A closer approximation of pi was achieved around 250 B.C. by the Greek mathematician Archimedes (ahr-kuh-MEED-eez) of Syracuse, who calculated pi to be between $\frac{223}{71}$ and $\frac{22}{7}$. This is very close to the value known for pi today, which is approximately 3.14159. For simplicity's sake, we usually use the number 3.14.

The Rhind Papyrus, written around 1650 B.C. by an Egyptian scribe named Ahmes, contains the earliest known reference to pi.

Let's say that the diameter of a circle is 6 inches. What would be the circumference? Use the knowledge that you have of circles and pi to solve this problem. Since we know that the circumference of a cirlce is equal to pi times the diameter, we can set up an equation using π as 3.14.

C = πd
d = 6 inches   π = 3.14

C = 3.14 x 6
C = 18.84 inches

The circumference would equal 18.84 inches

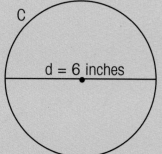

7

Circles are everywhere. Clocks, bicycle wheels, CDs, and Ferris wheels are all circles. All circles are divided into 360 degrees. Why 360 degrees? We must thank the ancient people of Babylon for determining that circles can be divided into 360 equal parts.

There are several explanations for how the Babylonians chose this number. One explanation can be found in a Babylonian measurement of distance called the *Babylonian mile*. This was a very long distance equivalent to about 7 of our miles (11.3 km). The Babylonian mile also became known as a way of measuring time—namely the time required to travel 1 Babylonian mile. This unit of time was called the *Babylonian time-mile*. This time-mile was further divided into 30 units.

One day or 1 **revolution** of the sun in the sky became equal to 12 Babylonian time-miles. Therefore, 1 complete revolution, or circle, was divided into 12 equal parts. Since the Babylonian time-mile was subdivided into 30 equal parts, we have 12 x 30 = 360 equal parts in 1 complete revolution or circle. These parts came to be called degrees.

Now that we know that a circle contains 360 degrees, how many degrees are there in a semicircle, or half of a circle?

Even though the size of a circle may vary, it always contains 360 degrees. The ratio of the circumference to the diameter of any circle will always be pi.

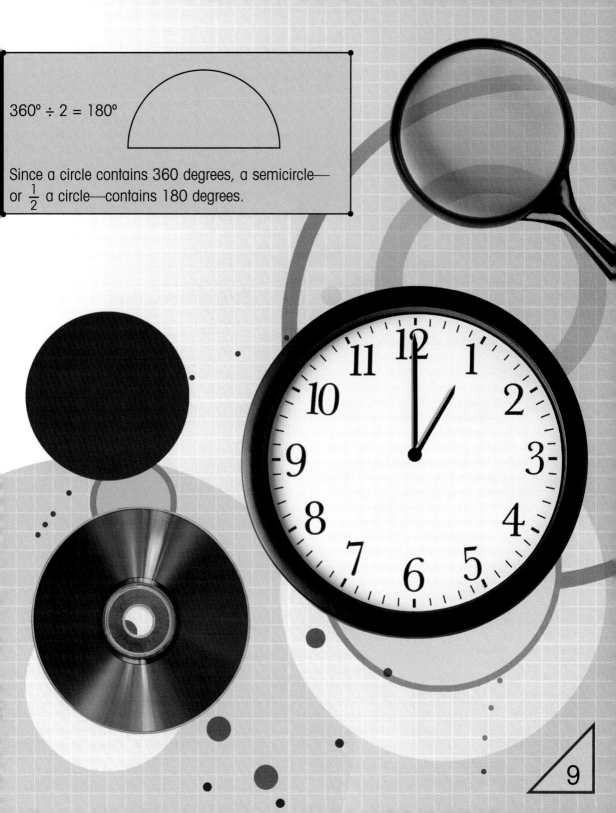

$360° \div 2 = 180°$

Since a circle contains 360 degrees, a semicircle—or $\frac{1}{2}$ a circle—contains 180 degrees.

9

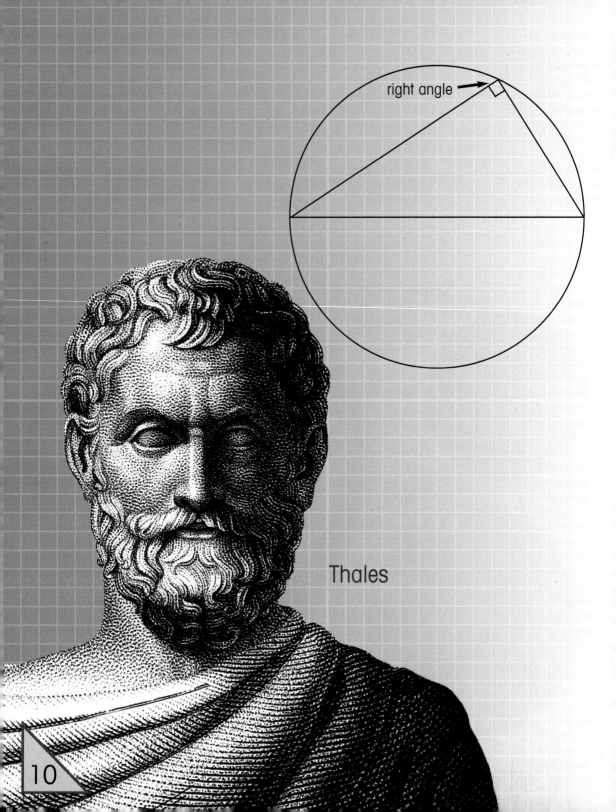

right angle

Thales

10

THALES OF MILETUS

With the development of new civilizations came a change in mathematics. Men began to ask "why" as well as "how" in regard to geometry. Thales (THAY-leez) of Miletus became one of the first mathematicians to investigate mathematical concepts beyond their practical use. He addressed the question of "why."

Thales was born around 625 B.C. in Miletus, Greece (now Turkey). Thales's mathematical discoveries marked a change in the way people thought about geometry. Thales supported his **theorems** using logical, **deductive reasoning** instead of using experiment. His method of proving concepts involved breaking down larger problems into smaller problems that could be proven true individually. If the many smaller problems were proven true, then it could be deduced that the larger problem was also true.

Thales traveled widely. During his travels, he studied for some time in Egypt, where he learned many geometric principles. There he calculated the height of a pyramid by means of shadows and focused his attention on triangles and their properties. Thales is credited with bringing the science of geometry from Egypt to Greece.

Back in Miletus, Thales became a statesman, counselor, engineer, businessman, philosopher, mathematician, and astronomer. Little if any of Thales's writings has survived. What we know about the mathematical contributions of Thales comes from the writings of other great mathematicians, who credit him for several key contributions to geometry.

Thales is sometimes known as the first mathematician.
One of Thales's propositions states, "An angle in a semicircle is a right angle."

In geometry, a triangle is a closed plane figure that has 3 sides and 3 angles. Each of the 3 angles is measured in degrees. The sum of the 3 angles of a triangle is equal to 180 degrees.

$a + b + c = 180°$
This is true for all triangles.

There are 3 types of triangles based on the measurements of the sides. A scalene triangle has no sides congruent, or no sides with the same measurement. An isosceles triangle has at least 2 sides congruent. An equilateral triangle has all 3 sides congruent.

| scalene triangle | isosceles triangle | equilateral triangle |

One of Thales's geometrical **propositions** states that the base angles of an isosceles triangle are equal. The base angles of an isosceles triangle are the angles opposite the congruent sides. The other angle is called the **vertex** angle. If the vertex angle of an isosceles triangle measures 80°, what would be the measurement of each base angle?

First, subtract the measure of the vertex angle—80°—from the total of all the angles of a triangle—180°.

$$\begin{array}{r} 180° \\ -\ 80° \\ \hline 100° \end{array}$$

Since we know that both of the base angles of an isosceles triangle are equal, we just need to divide 100° by 2 to get 2 equal angle measurements.

$100° \div 2 = 50°$

The base angles of an isosceles triangle whose vertex is 80° are both 50°.

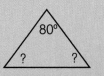

Another of Thales's propositions states that the sides of similar triangles are **proportional**. Two triangles are similar if they have the same shape, but different sizes. When dealing with 2 similar triangles, we know that the **corresponding** angles are congruent, and the corresponding sides are proportional. This means that if we know the lengths of the sides of 1 of the triangles, and one of the sides of the second triangle, we can calculate the rest of the sides of the second triangle. If $\triangle ABC$ is similar to $\triangle XYZ$, as shown below, what is the measure of side XY?

Triangles ABC and XYZ are similar. They have the same shape but different sizes. Mathematicians express similarity by using the following symbol:

$$\triangle ABC \sim \triangle XYZ$$

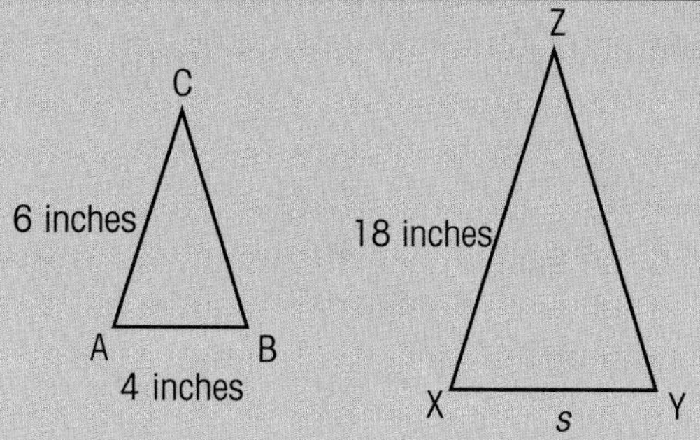

C
6 inches
A   B
4 inches

Z
18 inches
X   s   Y

Each side of each triangle is labeled with 2 letters. For example, the base of $\triangle ABC$ is AB. We can use these letters to set up a proportion, then fill in the positions with the actual numbers. The fraction on the left represents the bases of both triangles. The fraction on the right represents the left sides of both triangles.

$$\frac{AB}{XY} = \frac{AC}{XZ}$$

$$\frac{4}{s} = \frac{6}{18}$$

Cross multiply: $4 \times 18 = 6s$

$72 = 6s$

$12 = s$

Side XY has a measurement of 12 inches.

There are many ways to work this problem. Can you think of another way? Do you get the same answer with the proportion $\frac{AC}{AB} = \frac{XZ}{XY}$, or $\frac{6}{4} = \frac{18}{s}$?

13

Pythagoras

TURKEY

Aegean
Sea

Samos

Miletus

Sea of Crete

CRETE

PYTHAGORAS OF SAMOS

A Greek mathematician named Pythagoras (puh-THAG-uh-ruhs) was believed by many to be a student of Thales. He, too, used logic to deduce geometric facts from basic principles. Pythagoras was born around 569 B.C. in Samos, Ionia, in western Asia. In his early years, Pythagoras traveled a great deal with his father, who was a merchant. It was during his many travels that Pythagoras became well educated, studying under many learned men and philosophers. In Miletus, he met Thales, who contributed to Pythagoras's interest in mathematics and astronomy. Thales encouraged Pythagoras to travel to Egypt to study more about mathematics and astronomy. Around 535 B.C., Pythagoras traveled to Egypt and visited many temples and priests. According to some reports, Pythagoras was accepted into the Egyptian priesthood after studying with Egyptian priests.

In 525 B.C., Cambyses II, the king of Persia (now known as Iran), invaded Egypt. Pythagoras was taken as a prisoner of war and was sent to Babylon. While there, Pythagoras continued his studies with the priests of Babylon, learning about their sacred rites and perfecting his knowledge of mathematics.

Pythagoras moved to Italy around 518 B.C. and founded a philosophical and religious school. He had many followers, including women. A highly secretive society, they studied many mathematical concepts and contributed much to modern mathematics.

Around 520 B.C., Pythagoras was allowed to leave Babylon and return to Samos. Pythagoras soon journeyed to Crete, where he studied their system of laws. He returned to Samos and founded a school he called the Semicircle. There, Pythagoras and other members of the city held political meetings. Outside the city, Pythagoras spent many days and nights in a cave doing research and further study into the uses of mathematics. Unfortunately, the people of Samos opposed Pythagoras's teaching methods. Around 518 B.C., he left Samos and traveled to southern Italy.

Pythagoras's best-known contribution to mathematics is his famous geometry theorem, now known as the Pythagorean theorem. Although there is evidence that the Babylonians used this theorem 1,000 years earlier, Pythagoras may have been the first to prove it. It is important to remember that when Pythagoras developed what is known today as the Pythagorean theorem, he referred to a "square" not as a number multiplied by itself, but rather as a geometrical square whose side is also 1 side of a triangle.

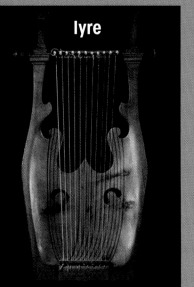

lyre

Historically, the Pythagorean theorem was stated in terms of area: The area of the square on the **hypotenuse** of a right triangle is equal to the sum of the areas of the squares on the legs. Today, the Pythagorean theorem has been changed to use the numbers as squares rather than geometric figures: In a right triangle, the sum of the squares of the lengths of the legs is equal to the square of the length of the hypotenuse. This is expressed in the form of an equation: $a^2 + b^2 = c^2$.

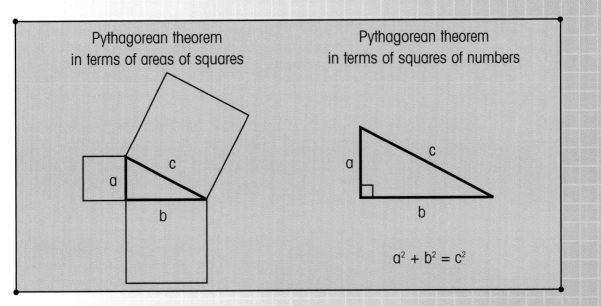

Pythagorean theorem
in terms of areas of squares

Pythagorean theorem
in terms of squares of numbers

c

a

b

c

a

b

$$a^2 + b^2 = c^2$$

PITAGORAS

Pythagoras searched for mathematical connections in many areas of life. For example, he discovered that strings whose lengths corresponded to ratios of basic whole numbers—especially 1 : 2, 2 : 3, and 3 : 4—made harmonious sounds when plucked together. Perhaps it is not surprising, then, that many historians believe Pythagoras excelled at playing the lyre.

Let's use the Pythagorean theorem to find the length of the hypotenuse of a right triangle with legs that are 5 inches and 12 inches. To solve this problem, we need to identify which angle is the right angle. This allows us to identify the other parts of the right triangle. Once we do this, we can fill in and solve the equation.

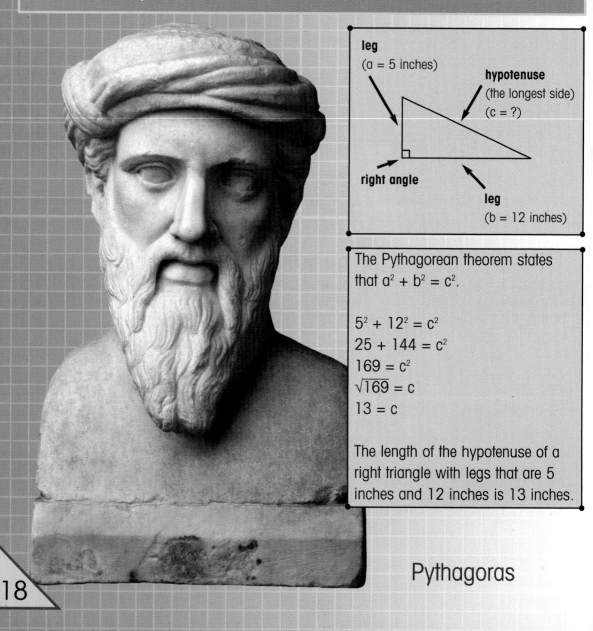

leg
(a = 5 inches)

hypotenuse
(the longest side)
(c = ?)

right angle

leg
(b = 12 inches)

The Pythagorean theorem states that $a^2 + b^2 = c^2$.

$5^2 + 12^2 = c^2$
$25 + 144 = c^2$
$169 = c^2$
$\sqrt{169} = c$
$13 = c$

The length of the hypotenuse of a right triangle with legs that are 5 inches and 12 inches is 13 inches.

Pythagoras

There are several other mathematical contributions attributed to Pythagoras and his followers, the Pythagoreans. One is the discovery that the sum of the angles of a triangle is equal to the sum of 2 right angles (90° + 90° = 180°).

Pythagoras and his followers are also credited with the discovery of irrational numbers. They did this by showing that the square root of 2 ($\sqrt{2}$) could not be written as a fraction in the form of $\frac{a}{b}$, as a rational number could. The square root of 2 to 8 digits is 1.4142135. However, there is no end to this number, and the digits do not repeat in a noticable pattern.

Therefore an irrational number, as discovered by the Pythagoreans, is a number that cannot be expressed as a fraction. Irrational numbers are infinite, which means they do not end. In addition, irrational numbers do not repeat their digits in a specific order.

pi = 3.14159265358979323 84626433832795028841971 69399375105820974944592 3078164.....................................

Pi is an irrational number because it never repeats its digits and it never ends.

EUCLID OF ALEXANDRIA

Euclid (YOO-kluhd) of Alexandria is known as the father of geometry. He is considered to be one of the greatest and most influential Greek mathematicians of all time. Little is known about Euclid's early life, but it is believed that he was educated at **Plato's** academy in Athens around 300 B.C. He remained in Athens until he was invited to teach in a newly established university in Alexandria, Egypt, where he founded a school of mathematics. He remained there for the rest of his life.

Euclid is best known for his writings, especially his masterpiece *The Elements*, a 13-book work of Greek mathematics and geometry. The long-lasting influence of Euclid's *Elements* makes him one of the leading mathematics teachers of all time. When Euclid wrote his books on geometry, he used 4 basic geometric terms.

A point has no dimensions. The dot we draw to indicate a point is merely a symbol of the point.	
A line has 1 dimension (length) and extends infinitely in 2 directions. Like the dot we draw for a point, the line we draw is only a symbol of a line.	
A plane has 2 dimensions (length and width) and extends infinitely in 4 directions.	
Space has 3 dimensions (length, width, and depth).	

The straightedge and the compass are Euclidian tools. A straightedge can be used to draw a straight line through 2 points. A compass can be used to draw a circle that has any given point as the center and passes through any second given point. The line segment between these 2 points is the radius of the circle.

In addition, Euclid gave 5 **postulates** that have become the foundation of Euclidean geometry:

1. The shortest distance between any 2 points is a straight line.
2. Any line segment can be extended infinitely in either direction.
3. A circle can be made with any center and any radius.
4. All right angles are equal to each other.
5. Given a line and a point not on the line, only one line can be drawn parallel to the given line through the given point.

RENÉ DESCARTES

René Descartes (ruh-NAY day-KAHRT) was born on March 31, 1596, in La Haye (now Descartes), France. At the age of 8, he entered the religious school at La Flèche in Anjou, France. He stayed there for 8 years studying mathematics, classical history, logic, and the traditional ideas of the Greek philosopher Aristotle.

After graduation, Descartes moved to Paris. From there, he moved to Poitiers, where he attended the university. He received a law degree from the University of Poitiers in 1616. Over the next decade, Descartes traveled throughout Europe. By 1628, he tired of the continual traveling and settled down in Holland, where he remained for the next 20 years. While in Holland, Descartes devoted his time to philosophy, mathematics, and science. He wrote many of his famous manuscripts, including *La Géométrie (Geometry)*.

Descartes was frequently in poor health and needed much rest. In 1649, Queen Christina of Sweden persuaded Descartes to move to Stockholm. She often wanted to discuss mathematics with Descartes early in the morning, which interfered with his rest. After only a few months in Sweden, Descartes died of pneumonia on February 11, 1650.

René Descartes is sometimes called the founder of modern philosophy and the father of modern mathematics. He is one of the most influential thinkers and mathematicians in history.

René Descartes, also known as Cartesius, made one of the greatest advances in geometry by connecting algebra and geometry. Prior to Descartes' time, geometry dealt basically with lines and shapes, while algebra dealt with numbers. Each was considered separate from the other. Descartes showed how to translate geometry problems into algebra. The union of geometry and algebra set the groundwork for the Cartesian **coordinate** system.

The Cartesian coordinate system is made of 2 number lines. The horizontal number line is called the *x*-axis. The vertical number line is called the *y*-axis. The 2 number lines cross at a point called the origin. Together, the number lines can be used to form a **grid**. Coordinates are an ordered pair of numbers (*x, y*) that indicate where points are located on the grid. The coordinates of point A on the grid below are (2, 6). The coordinates of point B are (–6, 6). Can you name the coordinates of point C and point D?

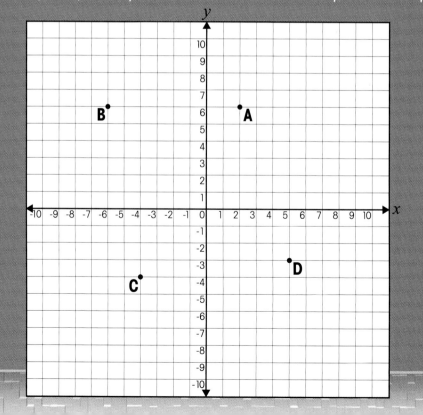

The Cartesian coordinate system allows us to create a geometric representation of an algebraic equation. Take the equation y = x + 1. There are many sets of numbers that can make this equation true: for example, (3, 4), (5, 6), (−2, −1), and so on. We can plot these numbers on a graph and draw a straight line through them. Any set of numbers that make the equation y = x + 1 true will lie on that line.

A myth tells of Descartes lying in bed watching a fly on the ceiling. He realized that the path of the fly could be described by locating points using the 2 bordering walls as references. This discovery established the framework for the Cartesian coordinate system that we use today.

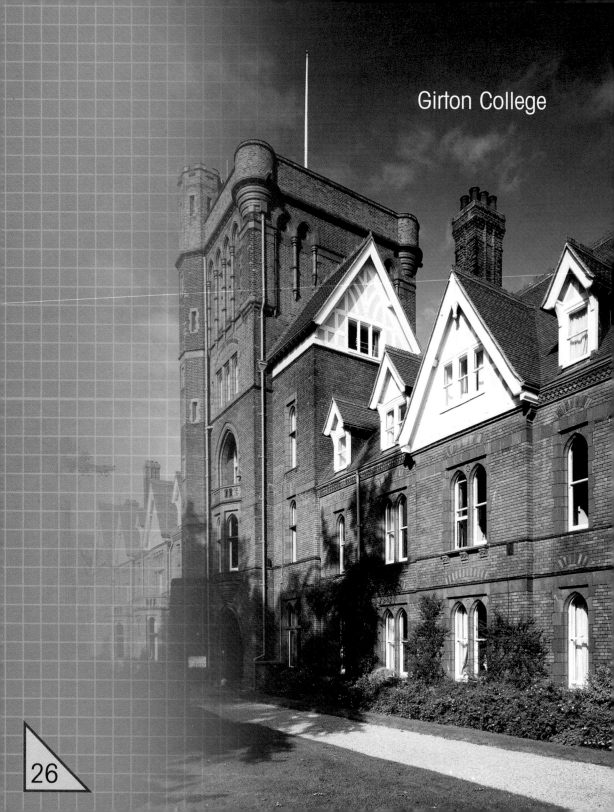

Girton College

GRACE CHISHOLM YOUNG

Grace Chisholm Young was born in Haslemere, England, on March 15, 1868, to Anna Louisa Bell and Henry Williams Chisholm. She was educated at home by a governess. At the age of 17, she passed the Cambridge Senior Examination. In 1889, she entered Girton College at Cambridge University to study mathematics. She received a degree in mathematics in 1892.

During these times, it was difficult for a woman to get an advanced education, but a new course of study had just been set up for women at Göttingen, Germany. Grace traveled to Göttingen to continue her studies in mathematics. She completed her education there in 1895. After graduation from college, Grace returned to England to take care of her parents.

Grace married William Young on June 11, 1896. Together, Grace and William had 3 sons and 3 daughters. Grace spent a considerable amount of time teaching the children while continuing her research in mathematics. She persuaded William to join her in creating children's books. Their first book together, *A First Book of Geometry*, was published in 1905. In this book, Grace used paper folding to teach young children concepts in geometry. "Nets," as she called the patterns, helped children to visualize **3-dimensional** solids. By folding **2-dimensional** nets, children could create 3-dimensional shapes. Today, students continue to use nets as a way to visualize 3-dimensional shapes.

This photo of Girton College at Cambridge University was taken in 2000. The college looks much the same as it did when Grace Chisholm Young attended.

27

Here is an example of a net like those in Young's book.

This net will fold to make a cylinder.
Can you visualize the cylinder?

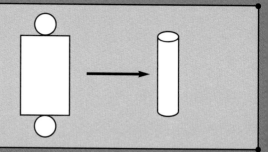

Can you use the nets below to make 3-dimensional models? Try this in a group by drawing larger copies of the nets below on large sheets of chart paper. What 3-dimensional figure does each of these represent?

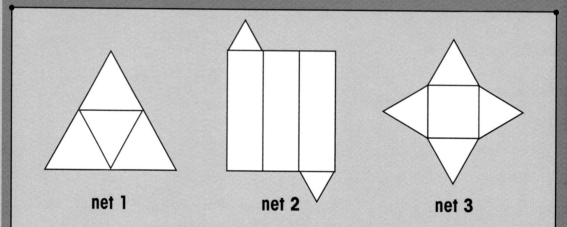

net 1   **net 2**   **net 3**

The nets above represent the following 3-dimensional figures:

Net 1 represents a tetrahedron, or a geometric solid with 4 faces.
Net 2 represents a triangle prism.
Net 3 represents a pyramid with a square base.

Many companies use nets to design packaging for their products.

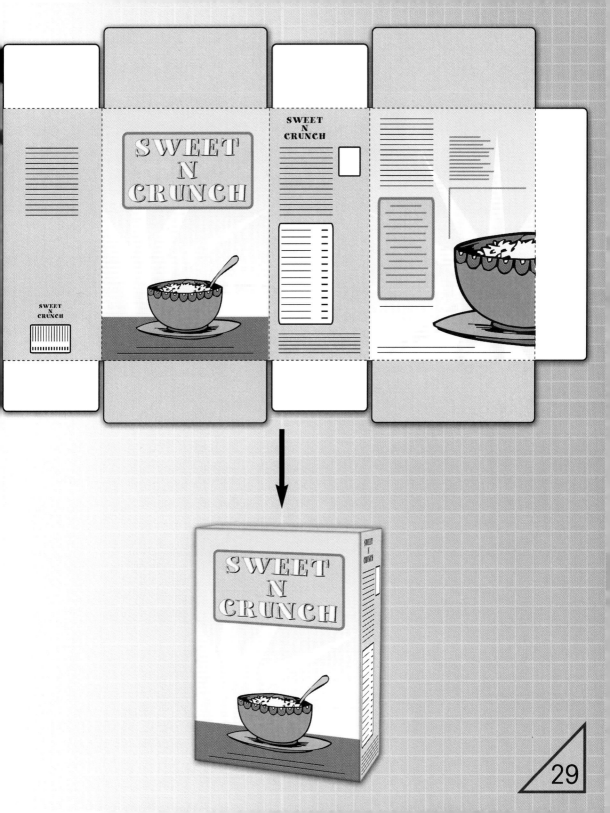

THE PIONEERS OF GEOMETRY

In this book, we have read about several mathematicians who contributed significantly to the history of geometry. The ancient Babylonians and Egyptians demonstrated a practical knowledge of geometry. The ancient Greeks practiced experimental geometry like the Egyptians and Babylonians did. Over the ages, geometry grew from this use of basic measurements to the deductive reasoning and geometry of Thales. Thales elevated measurements from practical applications—the "how"—to philosophical logic—the "why." Geometry continued to change as new discoveries came from the work of Pythagoras, Euclid, and Archimedes. Descartes united the mathematics of geometry and algebra to form a new branch of study. Grace Chisholm Young showed that 3-dimensional solids could be represented in 2-dimensional forms.

Many others have contributed to the development and growth of the study of geometry. Why have so many mathematicians been interested in geometry? Look around you, and you'll see geometry everywhere. Windows are often rectangles, the path of a fan blade is a circle, and nets are used to create things like cereal boxes. Modern buildings are often based on the repetition of basic geometric shapes. Without knowledge of geometry, the world we live in would be a very different place.

GLOSSARY

circumference (suhr-KUHM-fuh-ruhns) The perimeter of a circle.

coordinate (koh-OHRD-nuht) One of 2 numbers that indicate where a point appears on a plane.

corresponding (kohr-uh-SPAHN-ding) In the same position.

deductive reasoning (dih-DUHK-tihv REE-suhn-ing) Using known facts to reach logical conclusions that can easily be proven.

grid (GRIHD) A network of evenly spaced horizontal and vertical lines.

hypotenuse (hy-PAH-tuh-noos) The longest side of a right triangle. The hypotenuse is the side opposite the right angle.

isosceles triangle (i-SAHS-leez TRY-an-guhl) A triangle with 2 equal sides.

Plato (PLAYT-oh) A Greek philosopher who lived from 428 B.C. to about 347 B.C.

polygon (PAH-lee-gahn) A closed plane figure with straight lines for sides.

postulate (PAHS-chuh-luht) An essential idea upon which reasoning is based.

proportional (pruh-POHR-shuh-nuhl) Having the same ratio.

proposition (prah-puh-ZIH-shun) A theorem that can be demonstrated.

revolution (reh-vuh-LOO-shun) Completion of 1 full circle.

right triangle (RYT TRY-an-guhl) A triangle with a 90° angle.

theorem (THEER-uhm) A mathematical formula or statement.

3-dimensional (THREE–duh-MEHN-shuh-nuhl) Having height, width, and depth.

2-dimensional (TOO–duh-MEHN-shuh-nuhl) Having height and width.

vertex (VUHR-teks) The angle opposite to and farthest from the base of an isosceles triangle.

INDEX

A

Archimedes, 6, 30

B

Babylon(ian), 4, 6, 8, 15, 16
Babylonians, 4, 6, 8, 16, 30
base angles, 12

C

Cartesian coordinate system, 24, 25
circle(s), 4, 6, 7, 8, 9, 30

D

deductive reasoning, 11
Descartes, René, 23, 24, 30

E

Egypt(ian), 4, 6, 11, 15, 20
Egyptians, 4, 6, 30
Elements, The, 20
equilateral triangle, 12
Euclid, 20, 21, 30

F

First Book of Geometry, A, 27

G

Géométrie, La, 23
Greece, 11
Greek(s), 6, 15, 20, 23, 30

H

hypotenuse, 16, 18

I

irrational number(s), 19
isosceles triangle(s), 4, 12

N

net(s), 27, 28, 30

P

pi, 6, 7
Plato, 20
Pythagoras, 15, 16, 19, 30
Pythagoreans, 19
Pythagorean theorem, 16, 17, 18

R

right triangle(s), 4, 16, 18

S

scalene triangle, 12
Semicircle, 16

T

Thales, 11, 12, 13, 15, 30

V

vertex, 12

Y

Young, Grace Chisholm, 27, 28, 30